Something happened to me

written by Phyllis E. Sweet
illustrated by Barbara Lindquist
coordinated by Jeanne Arnold

and dedicated
to those who have been robbed of their childhood innocence
and to all our children who have the right to receive love and protection.

Published by Mother Courage Press

Copyright 1981 by Phyllis E. Sweet
Illustrations copyright 1981 by Barbara Lindquist
All rights reserved
Library of Congress number 81-83422
ISBN 0-941300-00-5

Mother Courage Press
1533 Illinois Street
Racine, WI 53405

"But the young, young children, O my brothers,
They are weeping bitterly!
They are weeping in the playtime of the others
In the country of the free."

Elizabeth Barrett Browning
"The Cry of the Children"

Introduction

Are the incidences of sexual abuse of children increasing? Estimates run from one in twenty to one in four children who have experienced this trauma. But statistics are questionable because they are based only on reported cases.

However, public awareness of the problem and the need for prevention and treatment of sexually abused children is growing, yet the funding for mental health programs is diminishing.

Frustration with the severity of this problem combined with the lack of materials available for use with the children are the reasons this book was written. Clearly the incest taboo is not operating to prevent it — what is operating is the fear of discussing it.

Clinical experience shows that telling or reading a story often gives children permission to discuss their own experiences and to reveal their attitudes and perceptions regarding a "forbidden" topic. This book is an attempt to ease that reluctance in a situation with a sympathetic adult.

This book is not meant to be a simplistic substitute for in-depth therapy with the child and the family but a part of the repertoire of the skilled therapist. Its purpose is to be one of the tools that may help reduce the fear, shame and confusion of these children and restore their feelings of dignity and self-worth.

Please use with care and caring.

Something happened to me.

I feel different.

I'm afraid to talk about it.

I feel ashamed.

I'm scared.

I don't know what to do.

A person did something to me.

I was afraid to say *no*

    because that person might have

    hurt me or said I was bad.

I feel awful.

It could happen again.

Should I tell someone?

If I tell, what will happen?

Will they think I did something wrong?

Maybe people will be angry at me.

I will, I will tell

   so I don't keep feeling scared

   and like I should have a bath

   even when I've just had a bath.

I will tell

    so I don't have to be alone

    with that person anymore

    and maybe it will stop.

I wish I had a fairy godmother

who would make it all go away.

But I don't.

I'd better find a real person to tell.

I did tell.

For a while I thought

they didn't believe me,

but they did.

They felt bad, too.

They took care of me.

They took me to see someone.

We talked about what happened.

We talked about what's good and what isn't.

We talked about watching that's fun

　like watching a spider spinning a web

　or watching an airplane looping the loop.

We talked about watching things that make you feel strange

　like grown-up, private things

　that maybe you don't really want to see.

We talked about touching that feels good

   like hugging and rocking and cuddling.

We talked about touching that you don't like —

   like hitting . . .

   or touching in places that make you feel strange,

   touching when you're half asleep and pretending not to know,

   touching that someone tells you *not* to talk about.

We talked about feeling good about your body and why

   what happened didn't make me feel good at all,

   mostly because I didn't want to do it.

Even though I got extra presents

   and sometimes money

   and got to stay up late,

   it just didn't feel right.

When we talked, I found out

    that what happened to me was not my fault

    and that it sometimes happens to other kids too.

I found out that no one has a right

    to do things like that to me.

Sometimes some grown-ups get very mixed up

    and do things they shouldn't.

They need help too.

Something happened to me.

I still don't feel right about it, but

    I know I will get better.

Now I know that I am a special and good person.

If something bad happens to you, don't think

   you're the only one or that something is wrong with you.

Tell someone so that they can try to help you,

   so that you can talk and not feel so scared and alone.

And then you can begin to think about who loves you

   and who can help you know

   that you are a special and good person too!

Epilogue — To those who work with children

Warning signals that a child may be suffering from sexual abuse are not infallible nor is any one of them alone necessarily a positive indication. A combination of the following signals, plus your own intuition and expertise, should alert you to the possibility of abuse. There may be

- sudden personality changes in the child, either withdrawn or acting out behavior that is markedly different from previous behavior.
- unusual or pseudo sophisticated or seductive behavior.
- vocabulary or drawings that show more sexual knowledge than is appropriate for the age and cultural group of the child.
- excessive fatigue with no apparent physical cause.
- a family situation where there is an absence of appropriate or reasonable parenting and where one child is consistently favored.
- alcoholism in the family.
- a history of violence in the family.

Listen to the child. If a child confides in you about a sexual relationship, don't show shock or disbelief. Listen calmly and sympathetically. An appropriate reaction is one that is similar to the way you would react if the child told you about being badly hurt in any other way.

If you are not an experienced therapist, seek consultation. Family dynamics and the reactions of the individual child are complex and sometimes puzzling and unpredictable.

It is important not to exacerbate painful feelings by blaming, and it is vital to remember that the child is a part of a family system and needs to continue functioning as part of that system no matter what protective legal action may be taken.

Therapeutic work must be done with sensitivity and awareness of the complexities. The child may be confused and in conflict as well feel guilty and ashamed.

Do not hesitate to report the case to the authorities because of lack of proof. It is the legal system's responsibility to prove or disprove; not yours. Every state has a Child Protective Services division, or you may prefer to report to a sexual abuse center, hospital or directly to the police.

Reporting has its risks of damage; not reporting means that you are allowing the abuse to continue.

If the legal system is not working well in terms of protecting the child and helping the family, do something about changing it. You may

- talk or write to your state representative.
- mobilize the organizations to which you belong.
- write letters to the newspaper.
- enlist the help of the media.

People are not powerless unless they think they are, and systems are changed when people put time and energy into changing them.

Remember, this book is a tool. Its effectiveness is dependent on the user's encouraging the child to speak rather than to carry a guilty and fearful secret. It is not a promise that disclosure will necessarily ameliorate the situation quickly, but it is true that the support of informed, skillful and caring people can help.

Phyllis E. Sweet, M.S., is a clinical member of the International Transactional Analysis Association and a therapist in Milwaukee, Wisconsin. She spent twenty years in the public school system working with children ages three to twenty and their families. She has also trained educational and psychological staff in recognizing and treating sexually abused children. She has given workshops in various parts of the country and in Canada. She is currently in full-time private practice with children, adults and families. She specializes in working with survivors of abuse and continues to write and consult. She is the mother of three grown children.

Barbara Lindquist, who says she was a "professional parent" for 20 years serving as a Cub Scout den mother, Girl Scout leader, church school teacher and substitute elementary school teacher, has also been a teacher of children with learning disabilities and a director of religious education at the Unitarian Universalist Church in Racine, Wisconsin. She has worked in public relations doing illustrating, writing and photography, owned and managed a bookstore and is currently a partner and executive editor of Mother Courage Press. She is the mother of four grown children.

Jeanne Arnold is the public relations director of Milwaukee County Medical Complex, a major tertiary care teaching and research hospital, and partner and senior editor of Mother Courage Press. She has taught high school English and journalism and was a feature writer and news reporter for a daily newspaper. Her youth-related activities range from helping to start Racine's first Montessori school in the early 60's, leading church school activities at the Unitarian Universalist church and supervising college interns in communications and public relations. She is the mother of two grown children.